SCIENCE OF FUN STUFF

The Sugary Secrets Behind Candy

by Ellie O'Ryan
illustrated by Rob McClurkan

Ready-to-Read

Simon Spotlight
New York   London   Toronto   Sydney   New Delhi

SIMON SPOTLIGHT
An imprint of Simon & Schuster Children's Publishing Division
1230 Avenue of the Americas, New York, New York 10020
This Simon Spotlight edition September 2016
Text copyright © 2015 by Simon & Schuster, Inc.
Illustrations copyright © 2015 by Rob McClurkan
All rights reserved, including the right of reproduction in whole or part in any form.
SIMON SPOTLIGHT, READY-TO-READ, and colophon are registered trademarks of Simon & Schuster, Inc.
For information about special discounts for bulk purchases, please contact Simon & Schuster Special Sales at
1-866-506-1949 or business@simonandschuster.com.
The Simon & Schuster Speakers Bureau can bring authors to your live event. For more information or to book an
event contact the Simon & Schuster Speakers Bureau at 1-866-248-3049 or visit our website at
www.simonspeakers.com.
Manufactured in China 0417 SDI

CONTENTS

CHAPTER 1
Sweet Stuff

Candy! It comes in every color of the rainbow. You can find it in any flavor you can imagine. And it tastes delicious! Amazingly, almost all candies have one thing in common: sugar. But how can one single ingredient turn into so many different treats? And what makes candy taste so good? The secret is in the science.

To understand why sugar tastes sweet, start with your tongue. Those bumps on your tongue have taste buds inside them—and inside the taste buds are tiny hairs. A hairy tongue might sound gross, but without the hairs you wouldn't be able to taste. When you chew something, it releases chemicals in your mouth. The hairs sense the chemicals and send signals to your brain. That's how your sense of taste works.

Mmmm!

COOKIES
SWEET

PRETZEL
SALTY

LEMON
SOUR

SOUP
SAVORY

COFFEE
BITTER

Scientists have learned that people have around ten thousand taste buds, but only half of them work in adults. That means kids are better at tasting than adults! Scientists have also discovered five different tastes: sweet, salty, sour, bitter, and umami (savory). As they keep learning about taste, they might discover even more.

The funny thing about sugar is that
it doesn't just taste good. It also makes
us feel good. Sugar gives us a burst of
energy and sends happy signals through
our brains. Then our brains make us want
even more sugar. No wonder people love
to eat candy!

Too much sugar isn't good for our bodies or our teeth. Your mouth contains a kind of bacteria that loves to feed on sugar, and once it does, it breaks the sugar down into acids that eat away at tooth enamel. That can lead to cavities. Over time, eating too much sugar can even make people sick. It's okay to have a sugary treat once in a while. But the best way to get your energy is from fresh, healthy food instead.

Most of the sugar in the world comes from sugarcane, a kind of grass that is filled with sweet sap. After harvesting, the cane is washed at the sugar mill. Then it is crushed to get the sap out of the stalks. The sap must be refined, or made pure, so it is mixed with water and a chemical called lime.

This mixture is boiled to remove the clear, sweet juice, leaving all the icky stuff behind. Next, the juice is heated in special pans until sugar crystals form. These crystals are raw brown sugar. Some are then melted, cleaned, turned into crystals again, and spun dry until pure white sugar is formed.

Almost everything on earth is made up of tiny particles called *atoms*. When these atoms bond together, they form groups called *molecules*. If you look at sugar under a microscope, you'll see lots of box-shaped cubes called sugar crystals. The crystals form when sugar molecules are about the same size and shape. Sugar molecules like to stack together, and for that to happen, they need to be alike.

When it comes to candy, the size of the sugar crystals matters a lot. Smooth, chewy fudge is full of tiny crystals. Coarse rock candy is made of large crystals. Hard candy doesn't have any crystals at all. In fact, hard candy is so smooth and clear that it's actually a type of glass!

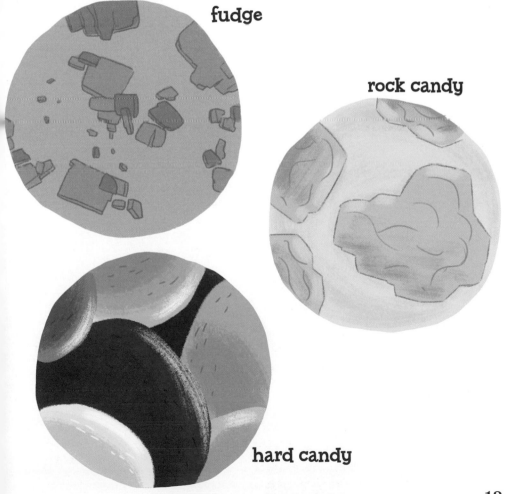

fudge

rock candy

hard candy

How do sugar crystals change size and shape? First, you have to make them disappear! It's not a magic trick, though. It's science. If you add sugar to water, the sugar crystals will dissolve. The sugary liquid is called a *solution*. If you keep adding sugar, you'll find that soon it stops dissolving. That means the solution is saturated, or full.

If you heat the solution, though, something surprising happens: You can dissolve even more sugar crystals in it. When a sugar solution boils, the water molecules break apart and evaporate, leaving a thick syrup behind. As the syrup cools, the sugar molecules start to stack up. Presto! The crystals are back.

15

There are a few simple tricks that help to control the size of the sugar crystals. Stirring a sugar solution while it cools keeps the crystals small, since big crystals don't have a chance to form. Another way to control sugar crystals is through how the solution is cooled. If you cool the sugar solution slowly, large crystals will form. That's how rock candy is made.

Cooling the sugar solution quickly makes the opposite happen: Crystals don't have a chance to form, resulting in smooth, clear, hard candy. Finally, adding other ingredients—like buttery fats or tart (sour) acids—also stops sugar crystals from forming.

CHAPTER 2
From Bean to Bar

Chocolate is the most popular candy in the world, thanks to the sweet skills of scientists. Like sugar, chocolate comes from a plant, the cacao (ka-KOW) bean. But the cacao beans that grow on a tree are nothing like the chocolate bars we eat. The beans are crammed into pods filled with sticky pulp. And they taste terrible! Cacao beans have a bitter chemical called tannin in them. To make yummy chocolate, the tannin has to go.

After harvesting, cacao beans are placed in sweatboxes, where a chemical reaction called *fermentation* happens. Tiny microbes, or germs, start to grow in the boxes. The microbes make oxygen and heat that help remove some of the tannin. They also turn the cacao beans brown and bring out their chocolatey flavor. After several days, the fermented beans are dried in the sun.

At the chocolate factory, dried cacao beans are sorted into different types. Each type of cacao bean has a slightly different flavor. One chocolate bar might use twelve different types to get the flavor just right. Next, they are roasted to kill any microbes left on the beans. Nobody wants to eat germy chocolate!

The heat from roasting causes two kinds of chemical reactions. One helps to remove even more tannin. The other reaction helps give chocolate its delicious flavor. After the beans are roasted, their shells are cracked open to get to the good stuff: the cocoa nibs inside.

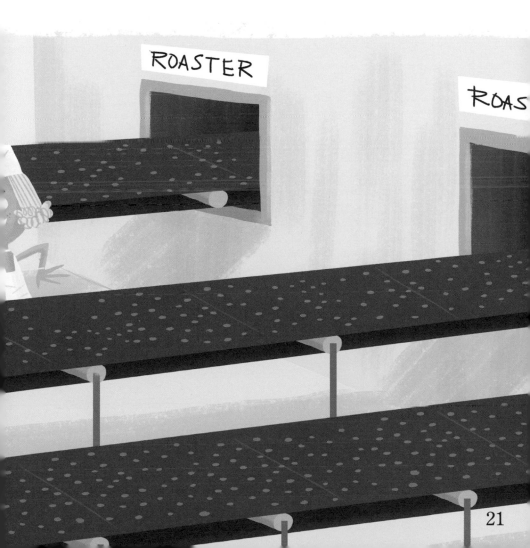

ROASTER

ROAS

There's still a long way to go before the cocoa nibs turn into chocolate. Next up, a machine grinds the nibs into chocolate liquor, a thick paste. Another machine uses so much force that it splits the chocolate liquor into two parts. Half of it becomes dry, powdered cocoa—the kind used to make hot chocolate. What's left is the creamy fat, called cocoa butter.

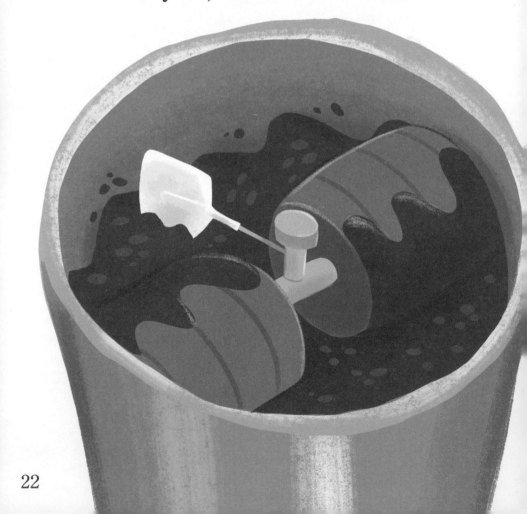

Some cocoa butter is used in soap, lotion, makeup, and medicine. The rest is added back to the chocolate liquor to give it a rich texture. Cocoa butter melts just below body temperature. That's why chocolate melts in your mouth!

At last, it's time to make the chocolate taste good. The most common ingredients added to chocolate are sugar, vanilla, milk, and soy lecithin. Chocolate makers often use the same ingredients, but each one follows a unique recipe. A chocolate recipe is a like a chemical formula. It explains which ingredients to use, how much, and how to combine them. Add more sugar, and the chocolate gets sweeter. Add more milk, and it becomes creamier.

The mixture tastes great at this point—but the texture is gritty, like sand. To make the chocolate silky-smooth, it is poured into a special machine called a *conch*, just like the seashell. The conch heats, grinds, and spins the chocolate to make it extra smooth and creamy. Rotating the chocolate in the conch also adds air to it through a process called *aeration*.

There is one more step before the chocolate is ready—and it might be the most important part of all. After conching, the chocolate must be *tempered*. Tempering is a special word for how to cool melted chocolate. When chocolate cools, it starts to form crystals—just like sugar.

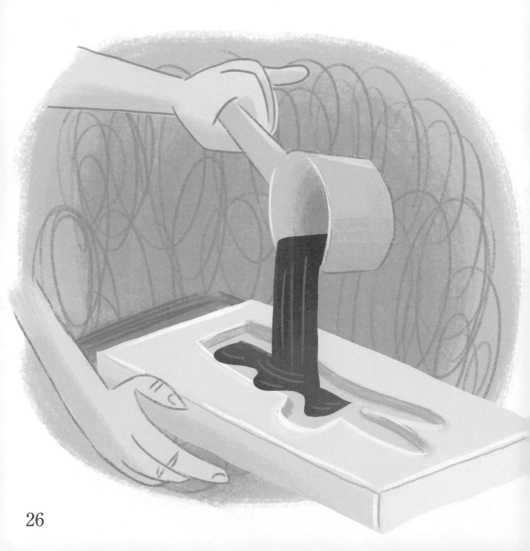

Chocolate makers use the tempering process to control the size of the crystals. Slowly cooling the chocolate through several steps makes sure that all the crystals are the same size. When chocolate reaches the right temperature, it is smooth and shiny. It can be poured into molds to make anything from chocolate bars to chocolate bunnies.

Chapter 3
Mouth Madness

Sour candy can make your mouth pucker up—just like sucking on a lemon! The secret ingredient that makes some candy so sour is the same chemical that makes citrus fruits, like grapefruit and lemon, so tart. It's called citric acid. Candy makers also use a different kind of acid for sour apple flavors. This is called malic acid, and it can be found in green apples.

The first type of citric acid was made from crystallized lemon juice. But it took way too many lemons to make enough citric acid, so scientists discovered a new way. Mold is a common type of fungus that grows in moist, warm conditions. When a type of mold called *Aspergillus niger* eats sugar, it makes citric acid. So if you like sour candy, don't forget to thank mold!

Have you ever eaten candy so spicy that it made your whole mouth burn? There's science behind that sensation! People often say that spicy candies taste "hot." But there's no heat involved—and our mouth doesn't even recognize "spicy" as a taste. There are two ingredients in spicy candy that make our mouths burn. One is an oil found in cinnamon that irritates the delicate tissue in your mouth. Ouch! The other ingredient is *capsaicin* (cap-SAY-uh-sin), the same chemical that makes peppers so hot.

When you chomp on capsaicin, it interacts with receptors in your mouth that sense temperature. The receptors are supposed to tell you if food is too hot to eat—not if it's too spicy. So it's a complete accident that your mouth senses spicy food as hot!

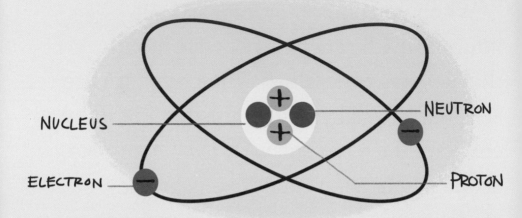

NUCLEUS

NEUTRON

ELECTRON

PROTON

Mint tricks your mouth too—by making it feel cold. If you chew on a wintergreen-flavored hard candy, mint makes something even wilder happen: a spark of visible light, right in your mouth! You see, molecules form when two or more atoms are connected by a bond. Each atom is made up of tiny particles called protons, neutrons, and electrons. Some bonds form when atoms share or steal electrons from one another. When you crunch hard candy, the force of your teeth breaks the bonds in the sugar molecules. And when a sugar molecule's bonds are broken, electrons fly free and crash into other molecules.

When the electrons smash other atoms, they make a spark of ultraviolet light. People can't see ultraviolet light, which sparks in your mouth whenever you chew on hard candy. But wintergreen interacts with the light so that you can see it. That's how you can make lightning strike in your mouth!

CHAPTER 4
Secret Ingredients

Candy doesn't just taste good to your mouth. It also looks good to your eyes— thanks to food dye. Food dye doesn't add flavor or nutrition. It just adds color. Some food dye comes from natural sources, like bugs, beets, or seaweed. But it's much easier to make artificial dyes in the laboratory. There are just nine approved dyes for adding color to food—but that's all scientists need. Just like paint, food dyes can be mixed to make any color you can imagine!

Candy colors aren't the only ingredients that come from a lab. Scientists can also make flavors. Natural flavors are often made up of hundreds of different chemicals. Wow! Usually a couple of the chemicals stand out more than the rest. By figuring out which ones have the strongest flavor, scientists can make an artificial version using just a couple of chemicals. It's cheaper and easier—and tastes almost identical to the real thing.

Some candy has another secret ingredient that doesn't add any flavor: gelatin (JELL-a-tin). It gives gummy bears their bounce and gummy worms their wiggle. Gelatin comes from collagen, a protein found in animal bones and skin. Cooking gelatin tangles up the proteins, making a jiggly treat that's fun to eat!

In your mouth, Pop Rocks feel like the opposite of gummies. They're crackly and snappy, not soft and squishy! Pop Rocks start as hard candy. After the sugar syrup is heated, carbon dioxide gas is blasted into it, making lots of little bubbles. As the candy cools, carbon dioxide bubbles are trapped inside. The hard candy is broken into tiny pieces—the Pop Rocks. When you eat them, the trapped bubbles burst. The "pop" comes from the bubbles bursting.

Carbon dioxide gas is also found in the bubbles in soda. If you drop Mentos candy into diet soda, the results are explosive: A fountain of soda will spray into the air! When carbon dioxide gas is added to water to make soda, the molecules form strong bonds. Those bonds keep the bubbles in the soda. Mentos might seem smooth, but they are covered in tiny bumps. The rough, scratchy surface is just right for breaking the bonds between the carbon dioxide and the water. Mentos are also the perfect size, shape, and weight to fall through the soda and break more bonds. When that happens, the bubbles escape—breaking even more bonds and creating the fountain. Don't try this at home without an adult—and an umbrella!

Science OF FUN STUFF EXPERT ON Candy

Congratulations! You are now an official Science of Fun Stuff Expert on candy. The next time you chomp on chocolate, lick a lollipop, or gobble some gummies, remember all the sweet science that went into making them.

Hey, kids! Now that you're an expert on the science of candy, turn the page to learn even more about candy around the world, and take a bite of candy history along the way!

Candy Around the World!

Everyone loves candy! Most people think of candy as a sweet treat, but some candies are super spicy, others are salty, and others are just plain weird. (Chocolate that's flavored with black pepper, cheese, or lemon salt, anyone?) Read on to find out about some popular kinds of candy from around the globe.

Pulparindo (Mexico): This candy is flavored with the pulp of the tamarind plant. Pulparindo is an interesting candy because first it's salty, then it's sweet, then it's hot. It's three taste treats in one!

Krembanan (Norway): Krembanan bars are jelly-and-banana-cream-filled chocolate bars—shaped like bananas! They were first introduced in 1957 and they remain unchanged since then.

Meiji Rich Strawberry chocolate bar (Japan): This candy bar is a deep berry-pink color, and you'll taste bits of real strawberry in every bite. Japan makes a lot of unusual candies. Meiji chocolate bars come in fifty-six different flavors—including the black pepper, cheese, and lemon salt chocolate mentioned above.

Japan also makes Botan Rice Candy, which is a lemon-orange candy that comes wrapped in edible rice paper. So you can eat your candy, and the wrapper, too!

Kinder Surprise (Italy): These treats are also known as Kinder Eggs and are popular all over Europe. These milk chocolate eggs contain a small toy inside. They are banned in America because the toys are considered choking hazards. So if you're curious, you'll have to travel to Europe to try one.

Elite candy bars (Israel): Elite brand candy bars are the bestselling chocolates in Israel. One popular product is a chocolate bar filled with popping candies (similar to Pop Rocks).

Violetas (Spain): Did you ever wonder what flowers would taste like? A company in Spain did, and created sugarcoated violets. These candies are popular in Spain, mainly in the city of Madrid. Some Spanish shops even sell these pretty and yummy treats in a fancy glass vase.

A Bite of Candy History!

Who made the very first candy? Historians can't say for sure. It is believed the word "candy" originally came from an ancient Indian Sanskrit word *"khanda"* which means "a piece of sugar."

When ancient Egyptians craved something sweet, they made honey cakes by mixing honey with dates, seeds, and nuts. And Greeks used honey to make candied fruits, stems, and flowers. The Greeks also discovered how to make syrup out of figs and dates. Ancient Roman candy was made from dates stuffed with almonds and stewed in honey to obtain their sweetness, but there was still no sugar.

So when did people start using actual sugar? It is widely believed that sugarcane juice was first boiled in India, and Indians were the first to discover and cook with brown sugar. When the Persian army attacked India in 510 BC, they learned about cane sugar, but kept its production a secret so they could profit from its export. Centuries later, in 642 AD, Arabs invaded Persia and learned the secret. After that, brown sugar and candy became worldwide sweets.

Over the next few centuries, sugarcane would become extremely popular in China. The Chinese began sweetening all their traditional desserts (which previously had been made with ginger and nuts) with sugar to create new sweet-tasting treats.

In the early 1600s North American colonists discovered that Native Americans had been tapping trees for their sap for hundreds of years. They would boil the sap in clay pots and had maple syrup and maple sugar long before Europeans showed up!

Also in the seventeenth century "boiled sugar candies" (what today is known as "hard candy") became popular in England. England was the first country to manufacture hard candies in large quantities. Soon after, hard candies like peppermints became popular in America.

Ancient Olmec civilizations of Mexico made the first chocolate drink. But the first solid chocolate for mass production was created by English candy maker Joseph Fry in 1847. Daniel Peter and Henri Nestlé from Switzerland created the first milk chocolate in 1876. And people started enjoying Hershey's chocolate bars in America in 1900. Candy became a booming market in America in the twentieth century. The future was sweet—candy was here to stay!

Hershey Time Line

It's known as "the sweetest place on earth." It's Hershey, Pennsylvania, where the Hershey chocolate bar was born! The candy bar and the town of Hershey are both named after their creator, businessman Milton S. Hershey. Take a quick dip into the history of the Hershey company with this time line of just a few of the Hershey company's accomplishments.

1857: Milton S. Hershey is born.

1876: Milton starts his first candy business in Philadelphia.

1893: Milton discovers the art of chocolate making at the World's Columbian Exposition in Chicago.

1894: Milton first experiments with making chocolate as a coating for his caramels.

1900: The first Hershey's milk chocolate candy bar is enjoyed in America!

1903: Ground is broken on the first Hershey factory in Derry Township, Pennsylvania.

1907: Hershey Park is opened. (The name was changed to Hersheypark in 1971).

1907: The first Hershey's Kisses are sold.

1941–1945: During World War II, Hershey's produced more than a billion chocolate ration bars for the troops.

1963: The H.B. Reese Company (maker of Reese's Peanut Butter Cups) is sold to the Hershey Chocolate Corporation.

1994: Hershey introduces its first white chocolate bar, Cookies 'n' Crème.

2016: Today, the Hershey Company has operations in more than ninety different countries around the world!

Being an expert on something means you can get an awesome score on a quiz on that subject! Take this

SCIENCE OF CANDY QUIZ

to see how much you've learned.

1. The bumps on your tongue are

a. Sugar   b. Amino acids   c. Taste buds

2. Chocolate comes from

a. Cacao beans   b. The ocean   c. Vegetables

3. When sugar stops dissolving in water, what has happened?

a. You didn't add   b. You need to add salt.   c. The water is saturated,
   enough sugar.   or full.

4. Hard candy is

a. A protein   b. An enzyme   c. A type of glass

5. What produces citric acid for sour candy?

a. Chocolate   b. Mold   c. Sugar

6. Tempering

a. Heats melted chocolate   b. Cools melted chocolate   c. Blends melted
                                                             chocolate

7. If you're eating spicy candy, there's a good chance it contains

a. Licorice   b. Capsaicin   c. Caramel

8. What makes gummy candies wiggly?

a. Gelatin   b. Air   c. Sugar

Answers: 1. c   2. a   3. c   4. c   5. b   6. b   7. b   8. a